POETIC INJUSTICE

WRITINGS ON RESISTANCE AND PALESTINE

POEMS BY
REMI KANAZI

Poetic Injustice
Writings on Resistance and Palestine

By Remi Kanazi

RoR Publishing, 2011

First published in 2011 by

RoR Publishing, LLC

Publisher@PoeticInjustice.net
Sales@PoeticInjustice.net
Booking@PoeticInjustice.net
www.PoeticInjustice.net

ISBN # 978-0-615-42166-7

Cover Art: Sean Basil McGiver
Design, typography, and production by Amani Semadi

For my Teta Leonie

You are my first memory of Palestine

Praise for Poetic Injustice

"Back from Gaza, Remi Kanazi's poems make tears come to my eyes. Poetry more than any other means communicates what is deepest in man, what gives us hope beyond crime and despair."
    —*Stéphane Hessel, former French ambassador and participant in the drafting of the Universal Declaration of Human Rights*

"It is through art not the news that we feel and begin to understand the long night of suffering and humiliation endured by the Palestinians. There is more truth, and perhaps finally more news, in Remi Kanazi's poems than the pages of your daily newspaper or the sterile reports flashed across your screens."
    —*Chris Hedges, Pulitzer Prize winner and Nation Institute senior fellow*

"Some poetry is meant to make you sit in quiet contemplation. Not so with Remi Kanazi's. Read his words out loud for yourself and your friends. Let their compassionate anger, their intricate dance of ideas, their unflinching witness, wash over you, dance with you, pick you up, and spur you to action."
    —*Ali Abunimah, co-founder of the Electronic Intifada and author of* One Country: A Bold Proposal to End the Israeli-Palestinian Impasse

"Repression creates resistance. It also generates beautiful artistic works, which become a cultural weapon in the struggle for the realisation of dreams. This book of poems is a shining example of tomorrow's Palestine."
    —*Ronnie Kasrils, former South African government minister, anti-apartheid activist, and African National Congress official*

"You want to hear a voice which refuses to be silenced, and only such voices carry the deep truth about what's happening these days, about what's happening in Gaza or Iraq or East Jerusalem? OK. If you do, listen to Remi Kanazi and the lucidity of his anger."
    —*John Berger, novelist and Booker Prize winner*

"Remi Kanazi's poetry, full of defiance and longing, allows us to feel the power and pain of Palestine's struggle."
    —*John Pilger, award-winning journalist, author, and filmmaker*

"In *Poetic Injustice*, Remi Kanazi lines up his word soldiers and marches into the battle of identity, occupation, loss, and exile. Stripping the spin and gloss from policies and politics, Kanazi volleys truths from his own life as a Palestinian-American and as a witness to the oppression and occupations, state terrorism, and racism. A poet with immense power and bravery, he underlines each phrase, word, and line with devotion."

—**Elmaz Abinader**, *author, poet, and PEN Award winner*

"With *Poetic Injustice*, Remi Kanazi has burst onto the scene with breathtakingly honest prose that shakes the reader's preconceived notions of the Middle East and pokes holes into the conventional wisdom that far too many people refuse to question. Run out and get this collection today—it will shake you up in a good way."

—**Cynthia McKinney**, *former US Congresswoman and*
Green Party presidential nominee

Acknowledgements

This collection could not have come together without the invaluable editorial insight provided by Michael Cirelli, Tahani Salah, and Carlos Andrés Gómez. Each cast new light on this volume, helping to shape the pages you find before you.

Also indispensable were Vinnie Gaetano and Yasmin Hamidi, who offered essential editorial consultation at every critical juncture. Both served as sounding boards throughout this process and provided paths forward when I found myself confronting seemingly insurmountable obstacles.

Special mention is also in order to the tremendous efforts of Amani Semadi, who skillfully and effortlessly crafted the design of this book. Her expertise and intuition transferred the vision of a manuscript into book-form seamlessly.

My heartfelt thanks goes to Andrew Felluss of Radian Records, who opened his doors to a first time recording artist and spent countless hours recording and producing the audio tracks that accompany this collection. Without his patience, guidance, and talent, this CD would not have been possible.

A number of dear colleagues and friends generously supplied vital feedback and assistance throughout this book's evolution and deserve mention: Rozina Gilani, Tami Woronoff, Giancarlo Vivenzio, Andrew Kadi, Achilles Yeldell, Sadie Vivenzio, Emile Saba, Frank Barat, Ziyaad Lunat, Dena Qaddumi, Phil Rigaud, and Adam Smith.

I remain indebted to my siblings, Ramzi and Rania, who persist in pushing me forward as a poet and creative thinker. Had they not taken me to my first spoken word show in 2004, these words would not have been written. I owe my deepest gratitude to my parents, who continue to give me the confidence to present my voice fearlessly.

Finally, I want to thank all those who have spoken up for Palestine, even as the current of society thrusts against you; history is on our side.

A Note to the Reader

Included in this collection are forty-eight three-line poems for Palestine. The number forty-eight denotes Al Nakba, or "The Catastrophe" of 1948, when two-thirds of the Palestinian people were dispossessed from their homeland by Zionist militias.

The poems are divided into four sections, each of which represents one of my displaced grandparents: Leonie, Spiro, Najla, and George.

Contents

A Poem for Gaza

I never knew death
until I saw the bombing
of a refugee camp
craters
filled with
        dismembered   legs
and splattered torsos
but no sign of a face
the only impression
a fading scream

I never understood pain
until a seven-year-old girl
clutched my hand
stared up at me
with soft brown eyes
waiting for answers

I didn't have any
I had muted breath
and dry pens in my back pocket
that couldn't fill pages
of understanding or resolution

in her other hand
she held a key
to her grandmother's house
but I couldn't unlock the cell
that caged her older brothers
they said:
we slingshot dreams
so the other side
will feel our father's presence!

a craftsman
built homes in areas
where no one was building

when he fell
silence

a .50 caliber bullet
tore through his neck

1

shredding his vocal cords
too close to the wall
his hammer
must have been a weapon
he must have been a weapon
encroaching on settlement hills
and demographics

so his daughter
studies mathematics

seven explosions
    times
eight bodies
    equals
four congressional resolutions

seven Apache helicopters
    times
eight Palestinian villages
    equals
silence and a second Nakba

our birthrate
    minus
their birthrate
    equals
one sea and 400 villages re-erected

one state
    plus
two peoples
    ...and she can't stop crying

never knew revolution
or the proper equation
tears at the paper
with her fingertips
searching for answers
but only has teachers
looks up to the sky
to see Stars of David
demolishing squalor
with Hellfire missiles

she thinks back

words and memories
of his last hug
before he turned and fell
now she pumps
dirty water from wells
while settlements
divide and conquer
and her father's killer
sits beachfront
with European vernacular

this is our land!, she said
she's seven years old
this is our land!
she doesn't need history books
or a schoolroom teacher
she has these walls
this sky
her refugee camp

she doesn't know the proper equation
but she sees my dry pens
no longer waiting for my answers
just holding her grandmother's key
searching
for ink

Palestinian Identity

I was born overseas
a refugee
with little knowledge of myself
or my ancestry

growing up in American society
I conformed to the mentality
I watched MTV
envied actors and people
who drove Mercedes
I didn't listen to Public Enemy
or read Edward Said
comprehend the need for autonomy
I was a dark kid
trying to be a white kid
acting like a black kid
in my middle class economy
but my mom didn't speak
this language perfectly
and I was reminded with certainty
my name wasn't Ali or Punjabi MC
not Khalid, Rashid
or anyone from Aladdin's family
I was just me

but who was me?
I asked the question quietly
as my relatives suffered
fighting oppression
in Mideast countries
what is Palestinian identity?
what was preventing me
from seeing what others
pointed out so easily?

it's scary not having autonomy
the only one with a permanent tan
on the baseball team
but it's funny being seen
I know, I look like the terrorist
in that movie
yup, the biggest nose
in three counties

but I think I figured it out eventually
I'm a Palestinian-American
standing proudly
with one foot on democracy
and the other seeking autonomy
while the media tries to rewrite
my people's history

I will always be me
with my roots planted firmly
American with Palestinian ancestry
planting seeds for hybrid ideology
in lands of productivity
you see these schemes
aren't just a dream
it's what I say
know
and mean

and one day
the truth will be seen
with transparency
so I step forward
a part of a team
the true essence
of what I believe to be
Palestinian-American identity

Flotilla

4 bullets to the head
    this is self-defense
they attacked us with white flags
    this is self-defense

we are a tiny state
    this is self-defense
we went through the Holocaust
    this is self-defense

we will sink the next boat
and the one after that
    this is self-defense

we must build new outposts
and a wall on their land
    this is self-defense

Haneen Zoabi is a traitor and a terrorist
Arabs must take loyalty tests
    this is self-defense

we can't recognize their villages
transfer to Jordan is needed
wheelchairs are a luxury
    this is self-defense

we killed 1,400 in Gaza
    this is self-defense

we dropped white phosphorus on their children
    this is self-defense

even when there is no defense
    this is self-defense

Home

I didn't grow up
in a refugee camp
I grew up here
comfortable
able not to know
or care
choose my own existence
close the book
turn off the TV
forget the stories

a gay man
once asked me
why do you
give a damn about Palestine?
why not?, I replied
why did men and women
clench fists
and fight back
at the Stonewall?
push through
Matthew Shepard
hate crimes legislation
in Congress?

I care about Palestine
for the same reason
I get emotional
watching *Schindler's List*

still can't comprehend
why kids in my neighborhood
picked on David
for being Jewish
was ten years old
the first time someone
called me a sand nigger
and I don't hate the town
I grew up in
but I don't forget
those experiences either

the way white women
on the block talked down

to my brown mother
don't forget the chuckles
pretend it didn't happen
don't feel the need
to dream up an alternative
American childhood
as if America's vision
ever intended to include me

people fight back
because they identify
my grandmother
still fills tear ducts
with longing memories of Yaffa
a home
we in America take for granted
I don't ask anyone
to forget about the Holocaust
or feel less Jewish
because they grew up on Long Island
not gonna have someone tell me
where my loyalties lie
because my physical environment
should define who I am

remembrance
is part of action
never again
applies to many peoples
I'm a product of America
but no less Palestinian

Palestine
being that fight
for freedom and justice
not just low valleys
beautiful sunsets
and fig trees
not just my grandparents' house
in Yaffa that's still standing
not just the place
I nervously visited
could barely catch a cab in Arabic
yet welcomed
like they were expecting my return

home
in the realest sense
I am Palestinian
I was born in America
that is who I am

Leonie

I have never seen someone love something so much. As if that something was a someone. A homeland, a companion. I didn't understand the need to return until I looked into my Teta's eyes

These are not rocks
They are the bulldozed
headstones of our forefathers

Missiles said, *With love*
I followed to where they hit
Charred limbs, stained tears, rotting corpses. No love in sight

She hadn't watered her garden in days. Can't water with bombs falling
Don't know how long the water will last. Don't know when the bombing
will stop. Don't know if her flowers will ever bloom again

From my rooftop
I can see an Israeli sunbathing
on the balcony my grandfather built

What do you say to a refugee
who barely touches life
but still whispers Yaffa?

A pregnant woman dies at a checkpoint
Sometimes a hand in the face
is as powerful as a pistol

෧

Her tiny legs dangled over her father's open arms like
spaghetti strings. Running blindly over rubble to anywhere
but here. One bullet in the stomach. The other still lodged in her chest

෧

Her fist snapped back like a slingshot. Raised it to the sky like Solomon's sword
Protested a wall that steals from her people, jails her brother, leaves homes
demolished. It will take much more than a bullet to unclench her resolve

෧

When they hoisted her onto the boat, she was seven months pregnant. Men were
careful, afraid she'd lose the baby. Two months later she gave birth. The
same day Israel claimed independence on the ruins of her village

෧

She doesn't want the American dream
or the Palestinian dream
She just wants to dream

෧

She closes her eyes. Smells the sea salt, caresses the soft sand, takes in a deep
breath, and feels the wind hug her arms as her father once did. For a split second
she imagines they have returned, where she was born, where she belongs

One Year Since

it's been one year since
I can still feel that first bomb

drop

every Hellfired
cluster bombed
city, town, and village
each explosion
                dragging
        a homeland
    back
one
more
year

I can still see little jovial girls
writing on missiles
vehicles
emerging from the South
on Israeli orders
white flags
running river red
with the stench
of charred flesh
and fresh suffering
images of old men
cupping seas of tears
on mounds of crushed homes
and limbs of children

I can still feel
my pounding heartbeat
and inner fear
no time for panic
a new war
old anger dredged up
balancing Iraq
Palestine
and Afghanistan already
raging against CNN and Wolf Blitzer
a Congress so filled with venom
a people perish

and my home country revels

it's been one year since
the Beirut blackout
and the generator
is still generating fear
not water
electricity
or sanitation

one year since
the death toll mounted
a world remains silent
forgotten
like the projects
and New Orleans
forgotten
like '82
forgotten
like all the forgotten
until the day
the forgetful
are forgotten too

Iraq ✓

Iraq
has a seventy-nine billion dollar surplus
we've spent more than a trillion dollars on this war
more than 4,000 of our troops have died
God knows how many are coming back limbless
others with post-traumatic stress disorder

this is not making us safer
this is not in our interests
this is what he says to me

an Arab-American
an American Arab
an American who happens to be Arab

I look back at him:
I'm not a CNN producer
and three Iraqis
have *died* since our conversation started

I'm not an American
I'm a human being
I don't write poems
about Kevlar vests or USO tours
don't get teary-eyed
every time I hear the national anthem

but don't get me wrong
I support the troops
the ones in Iraq
Palestine
Afghanistan
Northern Ireland
South Africa
and Birmingham

and not all of their bullets fit in guns
they've written music and literature
an oppressor could never dream of

I do
I feel bad
that I can't afford a new iPhone
but I've yet to hear you utter

that more than a million Iraqis
have been slaughtered in this war
that their seventy-nine billion dollar surplus
can't get them electricity or stability
that the surge has failed
Baghdad has been cleansed of Sunnis
and more than five million
have been made refugees

I'm sorry you can't afford
your cross country road trip
because gas costs too much money
and the US dollar
can't get you past Go in Monopoly

you wrap yourself
around fifty stars and lapel pins
while civilians in occupied nations
die because of US policy
if rejecting that
makes me anti-American
hood me
rip me from my home
and waterboard me
in a Guantanamo prison

I'm not looking
for the American dream
or your silly notion
of exceptionalism
you act as if
your so-called rights and interests
matter more than
the countless deaths of others

and you know what?
I'm not gonna call you a sellout
or Arab Uncle Tom
I'm gonna call you what you are
a shitty human being
one that chides the right
invokes civil movements
all while taking steps
backwards

yes

Iraq has cost us a trillion dollars
but there is no currency to replace
your thirst for hegemony
I'm not an American
I'm a human being

if that's so hard for you to stomach
maybe you should grab a plane ticket
with your frequent flyer miles
and move the hell out of my country

The Dos and Don'ts of Palestine

don't call it genocide
we don't want to offend anyone
if we offend them
they'll never listen to us
we have to be reasonable

1,400 is just a number
no names
no death
we want peace and negotiations

don't mention Zionism
if you mention Zionism
they'll call you anti-Semitic
and people will believe them

don't cite Palestinian sources
no one will believe you
I won't believe you
trust Israeli sources

don't ever be angry
if you're angry
they'll call you angry
if they're angry
everyone will call them
understandably emotional

we have to be pragmatic
pragmatism is not a euphemism
for concessions
although it may feel that way

don't mention Allah or martyrs
it reminds them of Al Qaeda and 9/11
it's not your job to fix their ignorance

don't talk about refugees
boycott
or a one-state solution
if we want to win
we have to compromise
the road to peace is just ahead

don't make analogies that include
the Holocaust, Nazis, or the Warsaw Ghetto
only Israelis are allowed to do this
when discussing wars on
Palestine, Lebanon, Syria, and Iran

don't mention Yaffa, Haifa, Safad
or where your family is from
but if you do
nod when random people say they love Israel
it doesn't matter where you came from
you can't go back

don't
just don't
and that will lead to doing

Before the Machetes Are Raised ✓

I'm disgusted by terrorists
backwards animals
who have no value for human life
produce propaganda videos
to disseminate their message
prey on the weakest in society
infect children
recruit fighters
like mindless pawns
in their ideological struggle

you know who
I'm talking about

soldiers
who drop bunker-busting bombs
on mosques and universities
decry the Middle East
but follow authority
closer than dictatorial rule
think stripes and codes
rather than decency and humanity
give them worth in this world

I've seen one too many Facebook invites
by jingoistic kids I went to high school
and grade school with
couldn't wait to get in some trigger time
hunt down towelheads and hajis
like venison

and when some marine's grenade launcher
catapults 120 mini bombs per minute
takes out seventeen houses
and fourteen schoolgirls
I'm supposed to feel bad
that he can't see his wife and daughter
on Christmas
respect his service
when he comes back to the States
a murderer who destroyed
a country full of daughters and wives
that'll never see Eid

we are so quick to honor our troops
but don't dare mention the widows
the trembling father crying
immersed in his wife's charred flesh
a fetus blown out of her stomach
the soldiers said
kicking down the door was too risky

where is the honor
for the 25-year-old Iraqi man
whose car was riddled
with American-made bullets?
pained face and surprised look
like grabbing for sky
falling out of 110-story towers

as long as we don't affect our interests
we'll shout out Darfur, Rwanda
and the need for antiretrovirals
look at people as aid packages
who can't compete
rather than ravaged lands
perfecting paradigms
of imperialism and propaganda

where's that right-wing Zionist
trying to save the Congo?
calling out Lev Leviev in Angola
genocide in Northern Uganda?

where's the humanity
before the machetes are raised
and proxy forces put into place?

King
Mandela
and Gandhi
aren't meant to be
conveniently referenced platitudes
to make Americans feel better at night
help us forget that uncomfortable poem
we don't want to face
we'll worship American Idols
but have no value for human life

and yet all I hear from twenty-somethings

is that "politics isn't their thing"
politics isn't *their* thing
when civilians in the Middle East
reach out for freedom and justice
they are defined as political
to undermine their suffering
creating notions of two sides
and equal conflict
covering up their dispossession
and burnt down villages

they are political
so we can ignore them
delegitimize and forget them

but they are human beings
gracing the windowpane
reflecting stillborn images
they are voices
chiming in choirs and temples
they are life
that won't be forgotten
they are the world's shiver
and whether you like it or not
they are coming inside

Spiro

Kids slingshot hip hop, mix beats, and break
in refugee camps. Reinvent art as identity
and tag the wall with the footsteps of their future

To exist is to resist
reads the graffiti
in their cities

My pain
is one link in a chain
of 62 years of oppression

This is not war
We write of life
It is the unfortunate life of war

You cannot
bulldoze our
minds

Free Palestine
is not a keychain
in your back pocket

I didn't come back for the mini-malls
or the randomly planted palm trees
I returned for Haifa's waves and Yaffa's oranges

In a café
with coffee and comfort
it is easy to compromise

Palestine is South Africa, Rwanda, Iraq, the Armenian genocide
and yes, the Holocaust, because if we lose sight of Jewish suffering
we become nothing but a reflection of the Israeli state

We will not be forgotten
left rotting like the food
you refuse entry

Injustice
fans the flame
of fanaticism

I am not a pacifist
but I find it easier to connect
the dots with a pen than with a fist

Yaffa

For my Teta Leonie

she no longer recognizes my face
never will again
but can still smell her oranges
feels the sun kiss her face
as if on her balcony in Yaffa
61 years later

described like the most magnificent villa
must have been seven stories tall
spanned half the neighborhood
tree branches opened like arms
so trunks could witness its beauty

I visited the house with my brother
Israeli cab driver said he'd never heard of the street
Palestinian presence must have made his memory fail

my grandmother was a painter
mostly landscapes
now she can only describe them
words like poetry
thoughts like a scholar
no matter how much I read and write
I always feel like a student in the presence of refugees

my grandmother's stories
came back like Haifa's waves
the outside world may never mention their names
but the roots of olive trees
will never forget what happened

Coexistence

I don't want to coexist
not like good guys and bad guys
in *True Lies* and propaganda
put on blackface as cabdrivers
or deli owners in your racist comedies
not bomb your Dunkin' Donuts
with my kuffiyeh
fist pound Fox News
or let you steal my food
and call it Israeli salad

I won't
Mess with the Zohan
or let him turn the rocks
of Palestinian children
into balloon animals
while Israeli soldiers
snipe our children's
heads, shoulders, knees
and stomachs
Hollywood snipes ears
of young ones
with lovable tales
of blue and white heroes

I'm not looking for your approval
not a token role or a job on my knees
scrubbing toilets in Israel's Congress

I'd rather fight
with Blacks and Latinos
against oppression
than concede to a
mainstream plantation
that sees me as Other
unless I'm checking
a college application

I don't believe in the tooth fairy
or 2,000 claims of homes
you supposedly deserve
from when people resurrected
and walked on water

I'll exist in a world that
fights against racism
like Martin and Malcolm
bleeds ghetto tales of Steve Biko
as a song that never dies
no matter what apartheid
makes of our bodies
feeds mouths in Belfast streets
and resurrects Bobby Sands' message
so that we will never
be hungry again

and whether you know it or not
I'm the best solution you have
one man asking for one vote
telling you to look at the sea
and I'll never drive you into it
I'll never return the favor

Religious Harmony

if I hear one more person
ask my religion
and think that one or the other
would shape and define
my worldview
I'm gonna flood his people
kill his firstborn
burn some witches
and have him drink
at a separate water fountain
because I'm a real Christian
turned perversion into pedagogy

this Zionist guy tells me
my grandparents were just
as persecuted as his grandparents
by the Muslims in Palestine

last I checked it was Jewish rifles
held against temples
that dispossessed Haifa and Yaffa
Haganah, Irgun, and Stern Gang
bombings and massacres
that formed an ethnocentric state
that didn't recognize
Muslims or Christians as equals

not gonna have some values preaching
hypocritical House Rep
tell me what's wrong
with all those Muslims
maybe I'll start listening
when he stops
starving Jesus' poor
aborting Black and Latino lives on death row
and overstepping homeless people
on his way into Whole Foods

and for the high and mighty liberal secularists
just because you don't call it a religion
doesn't mean radical capitalism
hasn't destroyed this nation
with your grimy bankers and bailouts
liberals didn't mind annihilating a country

when they thought they could do it on the cheap
implant a Starbucks on every Iraqi street corner
then blame George Bush when shit hit the fan

I don't know if this is a PSA or a poem
but I was raised Christian
and still can't see how that matters
hear Friday prayers
walking to the subway in Brooklyn
visit every quarter in Jerusalem
never knew religion by name
but had faith in my people
know that xenophobia is in vogue
and those who monolithically castigate
1.4 billion Muslims
are backward idiots
the true image of what they think the Other is
the actual ultra evil that has created its own axis
in which it fiendishly rules without knowing

9/28/09

today is Yom Kippur
it is quiet in the West Bank
they have shut down the borders
increased the checkpoints
birthday girls locked down
in prison cells

today is the eighth anniversary
of the second Intifada
fires burn inside stomachs
women sit in cold rooms
holding blankets
men cry like babies
remembering lost sons

it is 48 minutes
past my birthday
I can't celebrate
can't read anymore news sites
people will rally for Honduras at 3pm
people will die
because they can't afford
GlaxoSmithKline

my BlackBerry buzzes
message light blinks red
people are wishing me
happy birthday
I wish I felt better
I take it back
I wish them
those
the forgotten
there and over here
felt better
they need it
more than I ever could

a Palestinian once told me of his diabetic father
bounced from checkpoint to checkpoint
by Israeli soldiers who knew
he needed his medication
he died after one too many trips
just a matter of time

like everything in the West Bank

it is 56 minutes past my birthday
posting a new Facebook status
lighting 28 candles for Gaza
I am miserable in the Diaspora
wishing tears could replace
their stolen resources

my birthday began
67 minutes ago
I feel occupied
can't sleep
street light flickers
outside my window
quiet in Brooklyn
don't have to call it a cell
to be in prison

Najla

An IDF officer told me my pen was as dangerous as a rocket attack. Protesting
the Wall was akin to strapping a bomb across my chest. But to his vision
of a state, my presence is more dangerous than any explosive device

He lifted up his shirt, showed me two bullets that pierced his shoulder. Lifted up
his pant leg, showed me where a teargas canister shattered his kneecap. Never
touched a gun or picked up a rock; his loud voice, more powerful than any cannon

The soldier stroked his gun as he looked at the young girl. Raped her
with his eyes, occupied every part of her being. She said nothing. Stared
at the ground and kept walking. One more checkpoint until she's home

Stoned by Israeli settlers, a Palestinian boy lay bloodied on a sidewalk in
East Jerusalem. Dispatcher for the ambulance asked, "Is the boy an Arab or
a Jew?" The boy's mother, screaming in the background, said it all

They bombed the fourth floor. Said he didn't have a permit, said terrorists lived up
there, said the height was obstructing their view, said they didn't like the wallpaper
said and said and said. They bombed his neighbor. The family was still inside

In Gaza, an Israeli soldier remains in prison. The world knows his name and
the conditions to set him free. 7,700 Palestinians wallow in Israeli dungeons
The world cannot mention their names because it never bothered to learn them

After four years, he emerged from his prison cell. Put behind Israeli
bars for one rock thrown. Hit nothing, bruised no one
a casualty, like every heartbeat under occupation

Her brothers took refuge in a farmhouse. No fighters in sight. No
weapons inside. When the bomb blast came, it took over
three days to dig their bodies out of the rubble

They stripped them like animals
Took photos, traded laughs with brethren
High fives, dimples showing. Soldiers of occupation

They killed Anne Frank in Gaza. Hiding in the attic
Hellfire missiles transformed her body into ashes. Flames burned
her diary. Congress blocked her story. Only whispers remain of her life

Cluster bombs are like thieves in hideout. Robbers with one-way
tickets from America. Tiny bomblets harbor in the ground
waiting to steal the legs of playing children

Sometimes he gets scared to close his eyes. Claustrophobia overtakes
him. Pictures artillery shells pummeling the roof, trapping his
unmovable body. No one to help, buried alive

I Am Not Political

I am not
political

not a contentious issue
indigestible message
awkward discussion
frightening character
radical
or misfit

I am not
an ist or ism
not a neatly
fitted worldview
skewed
to serve
one people
or another

I am not political
not your
bumper sticker
campaign slogan
not an outburst
or sit-in
not a rally
or raised fist
I am like
all the other tragedies
you so meticulously
comb through
write reports on
build memorials for
and give Oscars to

I am not political
not partisan politics
a singular narrative
a rigid
immoderate
activist

I am the reflection
you think

you see
when you look
in the mirror
the anti-terrorist
the one who shudders
at the thought
of the destruction
of human life
from two towers
to two cities
in Palestine

I am the story
your children
whisper at night
the one
you can't seem
to remember
when making
calculated decisions

Not Said, Not Written

the soldiers don't stop
come up the ramp so fast
cars are lucky not to be
in their path

a woman
in the distance
makes slow gains
across the street

back arched
hand at waist
bulge exposed

there is a war going on
women shouldn't be
in the street
women should be at home
babies kept in houses
out of sight
out of their minds

when you hit someone
at that speed
body parts
become unrecognizable
limbs twist and turn
at the sheer force of impact
the up-armored Humvee
smashed her bones
like shattering glass
neck snapped
forehead collided
so forcefully against
eight thick inches
of bumper
that half her face
stayed glued onto
the metal frame
wasn't till he
jerked the steering wheel
that a long dressed body
tumbled underneath the vehicle
rear tire

diminishing anything left
of the baby

true story
just following orders
just following
policy not stated
just following
books not written
not said
not written
but happened yesterday
and last Thursday
just ignoring damage
on collateral lines
thin reports
from thick skulls
smashed her body
like planes into buildings

not said
not written
except on faces
in post-traumatic dossiers
on ropes
they hang from
on pills and shotguns
they swallow

heard about a man in Texas
blood spilled in our streets
white men that snapped
like that Iraqi woman's neck

our soldiers are not murderers
car bomb killers
doesn't matter if they bomb men in cars
they are not what logic says they are
not sinners
not losers
not criminal
they did not commit murder
their subconscious tells them otherwise
did not burn women and children in Fallujah
depleted uranium on steroids
did not make it snow in Fallujah

we fear chemicals on subways
those motherfuckers made it snow in Fallujah

soldiers snap
like necks of Iraqi mothers
Fort Hood, Texas
135 silenced themselves last year
where is Westmoreland?
can't blame Obama
can't blame Bush
too new for the ICC
too new to hood
and hang them
like Saddam
in kangaroo courts

shook my head
when those 220 stories
plummeted like stock prices
shook my head
when thirteen came out
in bags in Texas
shook my head
as they shoveled up what remained
of that mother and baby

not enough head shaking in America
probably too worried
they're gonna snap
their necks

A Letter

I'm writing this letter
to tell you that
I can't talk to you anymore
not in the way you want me to

we used to be partners in thought
hands outstretched
drinks thrown back
two peas in a pragmatic pod
if only others
could see the way we did

but now your face
contracts in grimaces
words you can't bear to hear
lines that shouldn't be crossed
too harsh for your parents
too normal for mine

I sounded like a bitter refugee
pined on Yaffa
emotions of my grandmother
talked of return and immediate action

I crushed our dream
with rocks of reality
a wounded dove
who could no longer swallow hypotheticals
when teardrops flooded Gaza like tsunamis

I read so much Chomsky
I didn't want to return
re-examined my identity
after Said's *The Question of Palestine*

finally recognized that
I didn't have to read a book
to be a humanist
Desmond Tutu, César Chávez, Rosa Parks
showed me the Right of Return through action

when I spoke of boycott
you dangled anti-Semitism

over my head like blackmail
and how could I shut down
my art to dialogue?
when I created art
to start dialogue
but Zinn told me
you can't be neutral on a moving train
King proclaimed
freedom is never voluntarily given by the oppressor
it must be demanded by the oppressed
and Adrienne Rich burned into my memory
the moment of change is the only poem

when I said we needed to act
you told me to write more poetry
when I said I wanted my poetry to bring action
you told me that my poetry was action

but I come from a family of privilege
a sector of society
that never puts its hand out
and writes policy for the have-nots
I tried to win hearts and minds
but found the keys to their hearts
were in their hands
opening doors to houses
they still carry deeds for in Akka

I'm writing you this letter
to tell you
I can't talk to you anymore
not in the way you want me to

but if one day
you want to meet again as equals
I'd be more than happy
to show you why old men
devastate backs and break bones
to harvest their land
a Mediterranean sunset
so magnificent
not even a settler's highest
hilltop could imagine its beauty
I can show you
perfection in bruised knees

the soft side of callused palms

I can't show you
in the way that you want me to
I can only show it to you
in the way
that it exists

Only as Equals ✗

every time I think of 9/11
I see burning flesh
dripping off the bones
of Iraqi children in Fallujah
now Gaza
I tend to memorialize the forgotten
the collateral damage
eclipsing America's unpunished crimes

maybe it's because I'm a numbers guy?
because if I had a dollar
for every time
an Iraqi died since 2003
I'd be a millionaire

and don't get me wrong
sometimes I don't know
who to hate more
the governments in the West
or the politicians in the East
who sell their souls
quicker than the oil they export
straw men who use Palestine
as a tool to line their pockets
and don't give a nickel
to their people
quisling governments
who stitch mouths shut for a check
from Washington and AIPAC
how can they be
Israel's prototypical anti-Semite
if they're signing peace accords
to oppress their own people?

then Orientalists and hypocrites
talk about how democracy
can't be allowed in the Middle East
because of what happened in Gaza
a Hamas bogeyman
wrapped in democratic elections
Rahm Emanuel wants to educate me
and my people
about democracy gone wrong
why doesn't he try

implementing one in Israel first?
instead of bowing down to terrorists
like his father and the IDF
lauding a third-rate, racist, European society
that's imploding faster
than its moral standing in the world
enlightened like 1950's Afrikaners
and slave traders
just because the house is beautiful
doesn't mean the bones you built it on
have fully decomposed

the Israeli left
is about as alive as Ariel Sharon
I'm sick and tired
of asking for permission to resist
from antiquated leftists and progressives
who care more about keeping it Kosher
than moving things forward

I put down my pen and waving fist
to resist with college kids
and Palestinians
boycott and divest
because who cares about
preserving a living
when governments
are killing civilians?

we'll boycott Elbit Systems
Caterpillar and your apartheid companies
we're taking back the right of return
and the keys to our country
because we never asked you
to go back to Europe
or sit in open-air prisons
I'm not asking for your advice
I'm explaining the decision

you can stay here
with us
but only as equals
it's not that you're Israeli
it's that you're wrong
that's why I fight for my people!

George

He measures time by cars. The checkpoint is 58 cars away, two minutes for each car. Counting is a game, helps pass the time. Sometimes he measures cars by length to estimate the distance. Too much time to pass, not enough time to live

I had a dream. In it, Handala unclasped his tiny hands, brushed off his tattered clothes, and turned around to face me. As he reached out to grasp my fingers he smiled. Together we walked toward the border and never looked back

Tell a refugee in Bourj el-Barajneh
that pragmatism is the reason
she will not return

Pushed back and forth like bodies on puppet strings
Checked at this point, denied at the other
Mice trapped in an ever-changing corridor of madness

A grimacing man peers through barbed wire, cocked rifle strung over his shoulder. His wife shouts below at children passing by. Throws buckets of water soaking their bodies. Soldiers see it all. Quiet as a winter's night

I am not from the Palestinian Authority
I am from Palestine
What Authority should I speak with to clear that up?

How do you expect
to understand the Middle East
if you refuse to televise their views?

🫒

A man in Gaza hides in a tunnel. It's the only place
he feels safe. It could collapse. A missile could strike
He thinks: one day I'll come out the other side and fly to the moon

🫒

I want to turn the page of a history book
Run my fingers across a map of Palestine
Feel olive trees grown back from roots

🫒

The garbage piles high in Gaza
The world's tolerance of human suffering
far and wide like the Mediterranean

🫒

He put down his gun to make amends
Not with Israel, but with himself. His right to resist
is unquestionable. But the method is of his own choosing

🫒

People say
Palestine made me political
I think it made me human

Workshop

14 faces
write, describe, paint
fade back
step forward
follow my motion
repeat her movement
open up
wide
vertical
show me

splash
spray crayon color on canvasses
invert your comforts
write
read, read, read

14 faces
mentor me
make me
write, describe, paint
make me smile
like little kids at Rukab Ice Cream

you are life
hiding behind
overcoming
running through barriers
clotheslined by flying checkpoints

little boy in Dheisheh
hardened this time
didn't see him since '07
time in jail pounding walls
for time outside throwing rocks

it is ok
acknowledge him
I'm just a voice
I'm from somewhere else
I want to be
here
I want to hear

your voices
open up
wide
vertical
show me

From Rikers to Bagram

1

an eighteen-year-old kid
was shot dead today
body faded into the pavement
his name was Malcolm
or Mohammed
or black
brown
blurred
boy

I can't remember his face
they never told me his name

2

forgotten faces
fill prison cells
in Rikers and Bagram
war-torn cities
collapse like Berlin Walls
opiates in Afghanistan
swallowed like the tongues
of Western correspondents

3

read about post-traumatic stress disorder
soldiers couldn't handle what they saw
but no one asked what they did
Iraqi whispers cut short
like hiccupped breaths
families left for dead
and stuffed in tents

makeshift refugee camps
always seem to expand
but never disappear

4

funny that we were the weapon
of mass destruction
found the day
our boots
our bombs
                    landed

cut with depleted uranium
and white phosphorus
sand found stuffed
in nostrils of lifeless bodies

5

an old man defecated on himself
shrieked in pain and disbelief
as he bled to death
didn't die like they do in the movies
sunburned while coagulated saliva
tangled with hot dry dirt
no ambulance in sight
no profound statement
or final goodbye

6

their pens
never touch history books
or update teleprompters
blue versus black and brown
they feel fear
when they hear the sirens
batons always seem to have
their names on them

bullets read:
Malcolm
or Mohammed
or black
brown
blurred
boy

I can't remember his face
they never told me his name
parents hugged the sky
hoping to feel him
once more

Us

Because every poetry collection deserves a love poem

I want us to work out
like bodybuilders
bond
like people awaiting trial
I want us to make it
like soon-to-be passengers
chasing after buses
live like kings and queens
and rewrite the American dream
as a love story
that chronicles our lives together

I want us to take that Chance
go past Boardwalk
and appreciate the Mediterranean
because it's not cheap
it's just the first stop
on our way around the board
in our race car

I want to take the periods out of the U.S.
and just have us together
suspended in a period
no one has ever dreamed possible
I want to write a poem about you
and talk about writing a poem
about you in the poem
because I want the audience
to know that I'm for real
and I've thought this one out

I'm not sure about many things
but this ring around my heart
is an engagement
trying to control the beat
so it won't burst
I wanted to write this for you
on Valentine's Day
but it's December
so I wrote this as a present to myself
I'm like an elf surrounded by giants
trying to reach up above their shoulders

just to whisper in their ears
how much I care about you

I want to have the courage
to give you this poem
stare awkwardly at my feet
as you read it
and hope by some chance
you look up, smile
and tell me that you feel
an ounce of what I'm feeling
that sunsets were made for us
stars were created
so we'd have something to look at
when our heads turned up at night

I want you to tell me
that we're gonna
write a poem together
and it starts right now
one of those forever poems
entitled:
us

Like Gandhi, Like Martin

I don't know if Palestine
just hurts more than it used to
but I try not to think of the kids
in Dheisheh anymore
great memories
tucked under pillowcases
more nightmares
brought by morning
blink images of live fire
at unarmed protesters
cameras spill out footage
of screaming mothers
born
bred
dead
in the West Bank
fought like Gandhi
like Martin
but no history book
will remember their plight

no one ever told me
it would be this hard
impossible to look away
after first glance
I cringe
every time someone
sends me more photos
dead babies missing foreheads
and frontal lobes
policemen lay still
lined up like dominoes
punctured chests
where organs once functioned
half a face missing in this one
an arm missing from that one
it looks like the bomb
beat his little body
into the ground

read reviews of our art, movies, and music
we're so angry, one-sided, never fair and balanced
what about *Schindler's List, The Pianist, Life is Beautiful*

and every other Oscar-winning movie?

never looked at Jewish pain
as something to conquer
never forgetting
that monsters once lived
under the skin of German men

we should be like Gandhi
like Martin
like someone else
pretentious armchair activists
who obsess over Monica Lewinsky
and Barack Obama's dog choice
if we all just rose up at once
like first Intifadas
people in the West forget about

wannabe feminists
peace activists
and pluralists
swallow tongues and gouge out eyes
wouldn't live this life for five minutes
but are too quick to criticize
the way we live it

the fallacy put forth
is that if Palestinians were only better
we would be free today
we should be better
than a people who happen to be Israeli
happen to be Jewish
because better is not racial
ethnic or religious
but situational
so for that
yes
we are better than you

we should be more like Gandhi, like Martin
and you should be more like F.W. de Klerk!
like Afrikaners admitting colonialism
and white supremacy in South Africa

funny that "enlightened nations"

always blame the victim
and never ask the needed question:
when will the day come when Israelis
and other colonizers of the world
better themselves?

About the Author

Remi Kanazi is a poet, writer, and activist based in New York City. He is the editor of *Poets For Palestine* (Al Jisser Group, 2008). His political commentary has been featured by news outlets throughout the world, including Al Jazeera English, GRITtv with Laura Flanders, and BBC Radio. His poetry has taken him across North America, the UK, and the Middle East, and he recently appeared in the Palestine Festival of Literature as well as Poetry International. He is a recurring writer in residence and advisory board member for the Palestine Writing Workshop.

CD Listing

1. Home
2. Not Said, Not Written
3. Religious Harmony
4. Like Gandhi, Like Martin
5. Yaffa
6. The Dos and Don'ts of Palestine
7. One Year Since
8. Iraq
9. Palestinian Identity
10. Only as Equals
11. Before the Machetes Are Raised
12. From Rikers to Bagram
13. Collateral Damage
14. Coexistence
15. A Poem for Gaza